THINKING ABOUT
RURAL DEVELOPMENT

World Development General Editor: John P. Reardon
Departmental Secretary of the Church and Society Department
of the United Reformed Church

THINKING ABOUT RURAL DEVELOPMENT

RALPH WHITLOCK

Former agricultural consultant to the Methodist
Missionary Society

LUTTERWORTH EDUCATIONAL
GUILDFORD AND LONDON

First published 1978

ISBN 0 7188 2299 4

Printed in Great Britain by
Fletcher & Son Ltd, Norwich

CONTENTS

LIST OF ILLUSTRATIONS

The author and publishers wish to express their gratitude to the United Society for the Propagation of the Gospel and to the Methodist Missionary Society for permission to reproduce illustration no. 7.

EDITOR'S INTRODUCTION

Ever since space-ships began to send back pictures of the earth we have realized the truth of the cliché that we all live in one world. Yet we have come increasingly to realize also that it is a world of deep divisions, none more tragic than that between the rich and the poor. Throughout history the conflicts within nations between the rich and the poor, the powerful and the weak, have caused political upheavals, social revolutions and much suffering and misery. Today those same conflicts, still present within nations, threaten the relationships between nations. Some suggest that the greatest single threat to world peace is the fact that two-thirds of the world's population live in conditions of poverty and deprivation.

The First Development Decade of the United Nations, in the 1960s, suggested that the problem of development for the poorer nations could largely be overcome by greatly increased aid from the rich to the poor, combined with economic growth in the developing countries. The conventional approach to development was through economics. Throughout those years the poorer nations increased their agricultural and industrial output, but in spite of overseas aid, largely in fact in the form of loans which they are still repaying, the gap between them and the rich nations widened. We no longer believe that the problems of the poor can simply be solved by the generosity of the rich.

The Second Development Decade of the 1970s, while still stressing the economic basis for development, has forced us to realize that there will be no real breakthroughs until we see world development as a process in which the rich and poor nations begin to recognize their interdependency and begin to see development in human and not just economic terms. More and more we are coming to see that the process of world development involves all the people of the earth.

Through a series of Special Sessions and international conferences, the United Nations has focused on many of the outstanding problems and challenges confronting the presently divided world community. Thinking particularly of the majority of the poorer countries, the UN Special Sessions of 1974 and 1975 addressed themselves to the acute problems, following the oil crisis and the huge increases in the price of oil, and issued a call for a new international economic order which would lead to a more just distribution of the world's resources, and would attempt to harmonize the interests of the rich and poor countries by speeding up the economic and social progress of the latter. Conferences like the World Population Conference of 1974, the World Food Conference of 1974 and the World Employment Conference of 1976 have given opportunity for governments to see the many dimensions of development and have underlined the fact that most of the development problems have to be solved by the world, rather than simply by the third world, community.

This series attempts to show how many-sided world development is. Each book deals with one aspect and explores the complexity of development as a whole, showing just how extensive are its dimensions. The series also attempts to show how the problem of development not only concerns what happens in countries far away, but has important links with and implications for our own lives.

Most of the world's great religions emphasize man's stewardship of the earth's resources, grapple with problems of evil and suffering and speak about peace and human brotherhood. It is, therefore, not surprising that religious education teachers have found themselves face to face with the problems of world development touching so many of the great religious themes. In their search for meaning in life pupils must face the realities of the world as it is, and must begin to see their own lives in relation to the puzzling and daunting conditions in which so many of their contemporaries throughout the world are growing up. We hope that these books will provide teachers of many subjects with a common basis and starting-point for co-operation in helping pupils to discover some links between history, geography, economics, culture, politics, sociology and religious studies.

John Reardon

AUTHOR'S INTRODUCTION

My chief qualification for writing this book is that I spent five years as agricultural consultant to the Methodist Missionary Society. During this period I spent much of my time travelling in Africa, India and tropical America (including the West Indies), inspecting and reporting on agricultural and rural development projects. Besides meeting innumerable peasant farmers in remote villages and listening to their problems I also made it my business to become familiar with any parallel or associated work in progress in the countries visited, from local levels to seeking interviews with ministers of agriculture and rural development. In the developed world I established liaison with church, charitable and government organizations in the United Kingdom, the United States, Canada, West Germany, Eire and the Netherlands. My information about what is going on is therefore unusually wide.

Before that I had had a long career as an agricultural journalist, a writer of books and a broadcaster on radio and television, and so was familiar with the work of the communications media. Perhaps most valuable of all, I had been brought up on a family farm and had spent more than thirty years of my life farming. I found that I could, as a result of this lengthy experience, meet the peasant farmers and villagers of the third world on their own ground, talking their language and understanding their problems. My sympathies were entirely with them.

It became evident to me that there were two basic and interrelated problems. One was to provide food for the human family, increasing in numbers at an alarming rate. The other was what to do about the illiterate, inarticulate mass of peasants who constitute the greater part of the population of the third world.

11

To solve the first problem is technically and theoretically possible — at least till the end of the century. Grappling with the second is much more difficult. At present, the task of feeding the 400 million people who have not enough to eat falls largely on the shoulders of these peasant farmers. They cannot succeed with their present methods and resources. Yet how can their lot be improved when the hungry millions for whom it is hoped they will produce food have no money to pay for it?

Supposing that large-scale modern farms were to replace the uneconomic peasant smallholdings and were to produce food more efficiently, what then would happen to the dispossessed peasants? Is there no future for them but to drift to the already overcrowded towns and add to the total of human misery and frustration there?

These are the problems which are exercising some of the best minds in both the developed and developing countries. In the following pages some of the main relevant factors are aired and discussed. There is always the chance that someone reading them will prove to be the genius who can point the way out of the dilemma!

SUGGESTIONS FOR FURTHER READING

Ward and Dubos, *Only One Earth* (Penguin).
Susan George, *How the Other Half Dies* (Penguin).
Towards a Strategy for Rural Development (F.A.O.).
The Food Problems of Developing Countries (O.E.C.D.).
Graham Searle, *Project Earth* (Wolfe Publishing).
Nance Lui Fyson, *World Food* (Batsford).
Michael Allaby, *Who Will Eat?* (Tom Stacey).
Ralph Whitlock, *Feast or Famine?* (Wayland).
Myers and Abbott (ed.), *Resource Guide in World Hunger* (Church World Service).
Lester Brown, *Seeds of Change* (Pall Mall Press, for Overseas Development Council).
Eric Jay, *Twenty Questions on World Development* (Christian Aid).
Food for Thought — A Study and Action Pack (Christian Aid, Oxfam and CAFOD).

1

THE PEASANT WORLD

When I look at the collection of colour transparencies which I accumulated on my travels in Africa, India and tropical America I have to read the captions to remind myself of where each picture was taken. The background and scenery are of little help. The dusty, khaki-coloured soil, the searing light that tells of great heat, the thorny trees, the eroded gullies are common to the tropical belt right around the world. The Indian, African and Brazilian peasant have much the same physical background.

These are, in general, overcrowded and impoverished regions — only a few are underpopulated. Their inhabitants, who comprise a big proportion of the world's population, have a very low standard of living. The average United Kingdom diet provides a total of over 3,000 calories a day; that of an average West African just over 2,000; of an Indian peasant 1,600. But many, of course, get much less than the average. Nearly 400 million people never have enough to eat. Most of them are in this depressed tropical zone. Each minute of the day and night at least seven people die of hunger and malnutrition.

Until recent times most human beings have lived in villages, or at least in towns small enough for them to be familiar with rural life. Now the pattern is changing. The new towns of the developing world are growing with the speed of an explosion. They are growing too fast for controlled development, and their imposing centres are in most instances encircled by a belt of appalling slums.

1. A village interior in northern Nigeria.

Africa

Tropical Africa can still provide examples of all phases of human social development. There are still men who get their living by hunting. There are still many nomadic tribes who follow vast herds of cattle on their wanderings. And there are innumerable villagers who cultivate the soil of their little *shambas* (homesteads). Africa still has space for these diverse cultures.

In Zambia, for instance, the human population is not really cramped. With an area approximately equal to that of France and West Germany, it has an approximate population of only four million — though it is true that there are large forest regions infested with tsetse flies. Elsewhere in Africa the pressure on the natural environment is steadily increasing. Wild life conservationists are worried about the future of Africa's magnificent big game. Although immense areas have been designated as game reserves, herdsmen, cultivators and poachers are continually encroaching on them. As one range warden put it to me, 'When the grass dries up outside the reserve and the tribes move in with their cattle, who will face those sharp spears and arrows in order to drive them out?'

Once West Africa had as rich and abundant a heritage of wild life as East Africa still possesses. Now that has largely vanished. Lions, hippopotami and other large animals survive only in reserves in the remote interior.

India

Overcrowding is far worse in India. There the human population has multiplied to the point of extreme discomfort and even disaster. Its villages have been settled for so long that every tiny plot of land has its own history.

India is a land of villages. One can walk the length and breadth of the sub-continent by dusty paths that link the villages, having always in sight lean-shanked peasants labouring in the sun-parched fields. Each is trying to wrest a living for his family from an inadequate collection of small fields. The land has been divided and subdivided through inheritance over many generations.

Any peasant one encounters is likely to be illiterate. His horizons are his own village and its neighbours. His life is regulated by necessity, tradition and custom. He will be able to direct a traveller to the next village, but ask him a question about the great land of which he is a citizen and he will probably look blank. He has never even heard of an entity called India.

He and hunger are no strangers. In a good year he and his family may just be able to manage on the products of their little farm; in a year when the rains fail they starve. As a rule, little food is available from outside sources, until and unless a famine is officially declared and relief supplies are brought in. But the local money-lender is there to help in just such emergencies. Most Indian peasant families are in debt to the money-lender, who charges such high rates of interest that they can never hope to be free.

North of the savanna zone of the old world tropics lies a region of great deserts. The largest is of course the Sahara, which imposes such a formidable barrier between the Mediterranean littoral and the mountains, plains and forests of the south; but similar deserts occupy vast reaches of south-west Asia and extend into India. The Sahara and probably many of the other deserts were once grassland, grazed by herds of big game. This could have been 20,000 or 30,000 years ago. Then a change of climate gradually desiccated them and introduced a regime of drought. Whether men helped to bring about that change by overgrazing with domestic livestock —

notably goats – and through wilful destruction by fire is not known, but it is certainly possible. Much of the near east has been despoiled by irresponsible exploitation and by goats. Greece, Asia Minor and southern Italy were once delightfully forested. The mountains of Lebanon were once covered with cedars, of which only one or two small groves survive.

Certainly India has been ravaged, and much of it is still deteriorating. It can hardly be otherwise – 14% of the world's population live in India. Every day the world's population increases by approximately 175,000 – that being the surplus of births over deaths. So if India had its level share of the increase it would be adding 24,500 to its roll of citizens every day. But India has more than its fair share. For one thing, it has a preponderance of young people in its population. The expectation of life of a man born in India today is in the low fifties (which is a dramatic improvement over the past thirty years). More than half the population is under eighteen. India therefore has a much higher proportion of women of child-bearing age than have the aging western countries. No completely reliable statistics are available, but it would appear that the population of India is increasing by at least 10 million a year. And the greater proportion of these new babies come to live (or die) in India's villages.

Many of India's troubles stem from the kindliness and humanity of the Indians. Indians love children. They love them for their own sake and also for the status they bring. A childless couple, or a couple with only one or two children, are pitied and in some instances despised. Furthermore children are useful about the farm: even a tiny child can herd cattle. Above all, sons are not only an insurance that the family name, traditions and land-holding will be perpetuated but are also a man's hope for his old age. He will have someone to maintain him when he is too old to work. Hence every man hopes for at least two sons. And, of course, some daughters are likely to appear as well.

An Indian farmer tries to be scrupulously fair to his sons. He does not apply the system of primogeniture but divides his land equally among them all. Moreover he tries to ensure that no one gets better land than the others. So his good land is divided into equal parts, and so is his poorer land. In villages where this has been going on for generations it is easy to see that the fields will be split into a mosaic of tiny plots. A man may spend half his time tramping from plot to plot.

Most Indian religions are pervaded by a sense of the sanctity of life. The most obvious example is the treatment of India's sacred cows. On no account must a cow be killed – although, incidentally, no one is under any obligation to feed her. Therefore one of the most noticeable features of

Indian life is the presence of innumerable scrawny cows, little more than walking skeletons, which wander at will along village paths or city streets. The tradition of reverence for the cow came into India several millennia ago with Aryan invaders from central Asia. When the Aryans were nomadic people on the Asian steppes, cattle were their life, and their leaders were concerned lest respect for these supremely useful animals should be lost under the settled conditions of India. So they decreed that cows were sacred, and the decree has been honoured ever since. But slavish, unreasoning obedience to the concept has destroyed the cow's utility. Starvation and indiscriminate mating have resulted in a race of cattle which produce neither meat nor milk and are an insupportable drain on the economy. For practical purposes the cow has been replaced by the buffalo.

Even more disastrous is the abundance of rats. In many communities they are protected under the general religious taboo that insists on the sacredness of life. At present they are estimated to number at least 8,000 million. If they could be eradicated vast quantities of food would be available for human consumption.

The prospects for India are less encouraging than for Africa because of these and similar Indian attitudes. India, the heir to an ancient civilization, has too much to forget. Africans, in many instances starting from a more primitive level, are less restricted by inhibitions and tradition. Once started on the path of progress, they are not hampered by religions which put the brakes on.

Central and Latin America

The situation in Central America is different from both Africa and India. Here several races and cultures are involved, each coping with formidable problems in its own way.

The West Indies when discovered by Columbus were peopled by a gentle, unwarlike race of American Indians, the Arawaks. They were soon exterminated by the ruthless Spaniards. Later the vacuum left by their extinction was filled by negro slaves imported from Africa. The descendants of these involuntary immigrants are now the main component of the population of the islands, the mainland coasts of the Caribbean and also of Brazil. Large contributions have however been made by whites, both Latin and Nordic, who have settled there during the centuries and intermarried. In some countries too, notably Guyana, there have been large influxes of Indians from Asia, introduced as paid plantation workers after the abolition of slavery. The population therefore is very mixed and, probably in consequence, highly vigorous and versatile. Most of the Caribbean and

Atlantic South American states have a mixed economy. In those which are primarily agricultural, such as Haiti, village life is at a fairly low level; but others, such as oil-rich Venezuela and Curaçao, are moderately wealthy, and tourism is transforming life in many of the islands.

The Spanish invaders found splendid and well-organized empires and kingdoms in Mexico, Peru and Central America. After they had destroyed these ancient regimes, the Spaniards freely intermarried with the Indians, with the result that vast numbers of people in the Latin American republics are of mixed Spanish and Indian descent. There are, however, many millions of pure or almost pure Indians, chiefly in rural areas. They are on the whole withdrawn, apathetic people, subdued by centuries of oppression and hunger. Their standard of living is low, and often they are half-drugged through chewing narcotic leaves to alleviate the pangs of hunger. Their ancient religious beliefs and traditions still survive through being incorporated into their special brand of Roman Catholicism, and such traditions, as they are concerned primarily with the agricultural cycle of the year, tend to dominate their lives. The village Indians are virtually untouched by the ferment of revolutionary ideas which are convulsing the cities of Latin America. Extracting a living from the meagre mountain soils to which so many of them are tied occupies their whole time and attention.

During the centuries of their rule the Spanish conquerors carved up their American empire into huge estates, many of which survive more or less intact. In many instances, therefore, the peasant villages have to operate under the difficulties imposed by an absentee landlord who has little or no interest in them. The same handicap exists in vast areas of Brazil, where the same system was introduced by the Portuguese.

Finally, the great forests of South America, and particularly the Amazon basin, still offer shelter to tribes who live – as their ancestors have always done – mainly by hunting, and who have had little or no contact with Europeans. In the past, when civilization has threatened to encroach on part of their territory, they have simply moved deeper into the forest. Now it seems that there will soon be no further hiding-place. The pressures of population and the search for wealth are opening up more and more remote regions. Some economists, whether justifiably or not, have visualized the Amazon basin as the last great unexploited larder of the world.

Village Life

The common denominator of these diverse peoples, in Africa, India, Latin America and also in the tropical lands of south-east Asia, is that they are all working in restricted village communities. Life for any individual is a perpetual struggle against adversity, ended only by death. A phrase in Moritz Thomsen's book *Meat is for Special Days*, about the peasants of Ecuador, comes to mind:

> 'They were celebrating the death of Crispin's firstborn,' I was told. 'He was born dead, an *angelito*.' There wasn't a bit of sadness in the town; it was a real celebration. Crispin's son had struck it lucky; he was one of God's angels without all of that intervening crap.

Not for Crispin's son the years of semi-starvation, the constant harassment of disease and parasites, the eternal drudgery of the soil which wore a man out before he was forty. He was to be envied.

Life was not so very different in European villages a few generations back. I myself was brought up between the wars in an English village in which we had no electricity, no piped water supply, no daily papers, no television, and no telephone. I can remember seeing the first car which explored our roads, and listening to the first wireless set. Everyone in the village gained his living from the land. Our lives revolved around the farms and were regulated by the cycle of the seasons. We ploughed; we harrowed; we sowed; we hoed; we reaped our harvest and carried it to the barns; we milked our cows and carted their dung back to the fields; we folded, marked and sheared our sheep; we plucked our poultry and collected our eggs. Our social life centred around the religious festivals, notably Easter, Whitsuntide and Christmas, and the Harvest Home Feast. We also made much of weddings, christenings and funerals.

When in later life I travelled extensively in rural regions overseas I found myself very much at home. Here again was the preoccupation with the soil and with the commonplace experiences of life – birth, marriage and death – with which I was so familiar. I could easily identify myself with these people. I knew only too well their joys and sorrows, their problems, frustrations and anxieties.

Yet although sometimes I feel I would like to return to what seems in retrospect an almost idyllic existence, I know that I would not like to cut myself off permanently from all the modern amenities I have grown used to. And I can appreciate the hankering of young people, in their dingy villages in Africa, India or the Andes, for a taste of the pleasures of the modern world. If I were an eighteen year old who spent all day turning over lumpy soil with a mattock in preparation for planting yams and had nothing to return to in the evening but a mat on the floor of a thatched, mud-walled, mud-floored hut, with only firelight for an illumination, I would feel a yearning for those garish lights of the city. I would dream of the day when I could work in a brightly-lit office or factory and perhaps earn enough money to buy a glittering motor-bike or at least a bicycle. I would like to have a pair of well-creased trousers and a sloganed T-shirt to show off my torso to the admiring girls. I would know that such things existed because I would have seen them on those infrequent occasions when my father allowed me to walk to the local market. One day I would manage to escape.

So the village boys dream; and for many of them there is never anything more than dreams. They are betrothed, by their parents, to a local girl who will bring as her dowry land to be attached to the family holding. They marry and immediately there begin the cares of family life. Thereafter their life is one long anxiety, coping with sickness, drought, awkward neighbours and the multitudinous problems of the peasant. Death at forty is a release.

Yet the present generation is conscious of an unsettling influence that their ancestors have not known. There is an awareness of the might-have-been. They know that some of their colleagues have made the break and have migrated to the towns. What has happened to them, in many instances, they do not know. The move may have been successful or it may have been disastrous. But, in any case, it could hardly have been worse than the endless drudgery that is the lot of the ones who stay at home.

So to all the age-old pressures of life in a primitive agricultural village is added a new one: the realization that there is an alternative. How to come to terms with this new challenge is the basic problem of the village communities of the developing world.

2

TACKLING THE PROBLEM

The Supply of Food

The problems of the hungry world have in recent years been the subject of innumerable conferences, experiments and projects, on a scale ranging from small local irrigation schemes to vast development campaigns backed by international funds. They need all the attention that can be given to them — and more. There are no facile solutions.

The basic problem is to supply food for a population that is increasing at an uncontrolled rate. The present world population is estimated at 4,000 million. Increasing at present by more than 65 million a year it is likely to reach over 7,000 million by the end of the century. That is equivalent to saying that each year from now to AD 2000 the world has to accommodate an extra country considerably more populous than Great Britain. Apart from the problems of housing, education and medical care, the world's food supplies have to be augmented by between 4% and 5% per annum. That would do no more than provide the present inadequate rations which about two-thirds of the human race have to exist on. Yet we are coming nowhere near achieving even this modest target.

The situation is much worse than global statistics reveal. The worst food shortages are occurring in countries which are already over-populated. It is in just these countries that the population is increasing most rapidly.

No permanent salvation may be expected from a programme of supplying the needy countries from the bread-baskets of those which are better off. The *total production* of grain produced annually by the United States, Canada and western Europe would be insufficient to meet the needs of the *extra* mouths calling to be fed within the next ten years – that is even if those countries kept back nothing for themselves, and even if there were sufficient shipping tonnage to transport such colossal quantities. Food can be and is shuttled to areas where large-scale famine develops, but this can be only a temporary measure. In the long term, it will have to be produced as near as possible to where it is consumed.

The major efforts of the more developed countries towards assisting the others in the matter of food supply have therefore been directed to helping them to help themselves. Apart from finance, in the form of loans or outright gifts for such major projects as irrigation dams, the aid given can be classified under four headings: technological help; improved varieties of crops (constituting what is often termed the 'Green Revolution'); improved methods of crop husbandry; improved marketing.

Intermediate Technology

Western aid to under-developed countries is generally offered on the assumption that it must be useful under existing political and social conditions. That implies that it can be used by peasant farmers. The tools and techniques offered must lead them on by easy stages to improvements in their present operations, not try to introduce something entirely new.

In the 1960s a widespread movement developed for raising funds for 'Tractors for the Tropics'. It was an attractive idea but did not prove to be a great success. More tractors than one likes to think about were soon rusting under mango trees in remote tropical villages, abandoned through lack of spare parts, or ignorance about how to repair or even use them. In innumerable African communities, once the possibility of obtaining a free tractor became known, they were sought after for prestige reasons by enterprising young men who had only the vaguest idea about how they should be used.

How much more practical was the scheme devised by a missionary and a Peace Corps worker in interior Sierra Leone. Here in the early 1970s the Japanese Honda iron horse was becoming popular, a small power-unit guided by a man walking, with sundry attachments for soil cultivation and other agricultural operations. It had the advantages of being light, easy to manipulate and therefore convenient for use in the small West African fields

2. A new Honda digger comes to an African village.

and for taking along jungle paths, and relatively inexpensive. So these two workers organized a three-month course in the use and maintenance of the Honda. In a practical test at the end of the course the student had to dismantle the machine down to the last nut and bolt, put it together again and then use it for doing a set piece of work. The students were selected from a wide radius of the bush, with the idea of ensuring that as far as possible every village in which a Honda was stationed should also have a man thoroughly competent to operate and maintain it.

Equally to the point, and perhaps more so at a more primitive level, was the action of an agricultural mechanic who, after a period of service in Nigeria, returned to England convinced that what peasant farmers of the tropics needed was not elaborate and sophisticated machinery but a range of improved tools that could be used behind oxen. So he designed a simple but efficient tool-bar to which a range of cultivating tools could be fixed. The implement was indeed admirable and much appreciated by the farmers who were able to obtain one, though it is to be feared that the invention languished since such a simple and inexpensive tool could not offer sufficiently attractive profits for the makers or distributors.

In 1966 an Intermediate Technology Development Group was founded in Britain (which has since become international) to provide a service for introducing equipment and tools for small-scale development to peasant farmers. One of its first projects was to prepare a guide or index to the range of simple tools then available. Pumps, ox-drawn harrows, knapsack sprayers and pull hoists are examples of the items advertised.

One of the simple but ingenious ideas mentioned in the guide was a small-scale rainwater catchment tank, subsequently tried out with great success in Botswana. In that drought-harassed country the heavy rains which fall from time to time soon dissipate in the hot, sandy soil. A traditional method of rainwater conservation is to scoop out a hollow in the ground, into which the water seeps. The suggested innovation was to enlarge such a hollow and line it with layers of plastic 'sausages filled with a mixture of one part of cement to ten of sand'. Over the top a butyl sheet was fixed. The improved tank had two main advantages over its predecessor, namely, its sides and bottom were impervious to water, and the butyl covering ensured that evaporation would condense on the underside of the sheet, the water dripping back into the tank. Thus virtually no moisture was lost.

To give an example in which I myself was involved, in a village in Mysore state in southern India I found the farmers using a heavy, inefficient type of harrow consisting of a V-shaped frame of timber into which iron spikes eighteen inches long had been driven. The spikes penetrated far deeper into the soil than was necessary, making the heavy implement more difficult for oxen to pull, and it took a course of only three or four feet wide in its passage across the field. I was able to show an intelligent blacksmith how to make zigzag harrows, of a type common in Europe, which with the expenditure of less energy would cover three times as much ground and make a more efficient job of the cultivation.

It is simple ideas such as these, which can be put into practice by peasants using little more than the skills and materials which they already have, that are of the greatest value.

The Green Revolution

Developments in the late 1960s seemed to promise new hope to a hungry world. Such spectacular increases in crop yields began to be recorded that the slogan *the Green Revolution* was coined. The wheat harvests of India and Pakistan were virtually doubled. Between 1955 and 1969 the average yield of wheat in Mexico was trebled. In Kenya and Zambia experimental crops of maize produced nearly ten times the average.

These splendid achievements were largely the fruits of progress in plant-breeding. In most of the more advanced countries plant-breeders have been improving farm and garden plants of all kinds by the progressive selection of the most productive specimens for more than a hundred years. As a result of their efforts we now have roses of exquisite shape, colour and scent in place of the wild dog rose; succulent orange-red carrots instead of the coarse, pale yellow wild ones; an incredible range of brassica plants, including brussels sprouts, savoy, kale, cauliflower, cabbage and kohl rabi developed from the wild cabbage of the sea shore; cereals yielding tons of grain per acre in place of the wild grasses from which they were derived.

In 1929 the average barley yield for England and Wales was 17·8 cwt per acre, the highest ever recorded. By 1964 that average had risen to 29·4 cwt per acre. The average wheat harvest for 1964 hit an all-time record of 33·7 cwt per acre. In 1929 a crop of 20 cwt would have been regarded as exceptionally good.

Because Mexico was one of the first of the developing countries to feel the impact of this benevolent revolution it was chosen as one of the main centres for the dissemination of the new seeds and new techniques to other nations of the third world. In the 1940s high-yielding wheats which had been enormously successful in the United States of America were transported over the border into Mexico and soon proved equally effective there. By the 1960s Mexico was producing three times as much wheat and twice as much maize as before, and from relying heavily on imports had become an exporting nation.

In that decade the organization of the Green Revolution became international. Four centres for agricultural research, training and outreach assistance were established. They were:

in 1960, the International Rice Research Institute, with headquarters in the Philippines;

in 1966, the Centro Internacional de Mejoramiento de Maiz y Trigo (CIMMYT), of the International Maize and Wheat Improvement Centre, in Mexico;

in 1967, the International Institute of Tropical Agriculture, at Ibadan, Nigeria;

in 1968, the International Centre of Tropical Agriculture, at Cali, Colombia.

To these have been added in the present decade:

in 1972, the International Potato Centre, in Peru;

also in 1972, the International Crops Research Institute for the Semi-Arid Tropics, in India;

in 1973, the International Laboratory for Research on Animal Diseases, in Kenya;

again in 1973, the International Livestock Centre for Africa, in Ethiopia;

in 1976, the International Centre for Agricultural Research in Dry Areas, in Lebanon and Syria.

Funds for the support of these centres and their programmes were initially supplied by eight primary donors, namely the World Bank, the United Nations Development Programme, the Inter-American Development Bank, the Ford Foundation, the Rockefeller Foundation and the governments of the USA, Canada and West Germany. To them have since been added many of the countries which are benefiting from the work of the centres, as well as several private corporations. The centres are autonomous and international, non-profit-making and engaged in both research and training.

To look in more detail at CIMMYT, involved as it is with two of the major food crops of the world: from its headquarters near Mexico City it operates a chain of experimental stations throughout Mexico, designed to give as wide a range of climatic conditions as possible. Elsewhere it conducts trials and projects in between 80 and 90 countries. In fact there are few countries outside the communist ones where CIMMYT trainees or research workers are not active.

Its plant-breeding programme is massive and continuous. It has germ plasm banks for both wheat and maize, from which it produces thousands of new crosses every year. In 1975, for instance, it made about 8,000 crosses in bread wheat alone. When a promising cross is discovered it is put through an exhaustive series of tests extending to six generations under as wide a range of growing conditions as possible. The aim is not only to improve yields but also the nutritional quality of the grain, by increasing its protein content. Resistance to disease and insect attack are considered to be factors of prime importance.

CIMMYT operates under the direction of the world-famous scientist Dr. Norman Borlaug who in 1971 was awarded the Nobel Peace Prize. In the same year CIMMYT and the International Rice Research Institute in the Philippines shared the UNESCO Science Prize.

One of the early successes of the International Rice Institute was the 'miracle rice' IR-8, which yields more than double the quantity obtainable from the old varieties. This has now been surpassed by even more productive varieties.

With maize, research scientists are now breeding into new varieties increased proportions of such amino acids as lysine and tryptopham, which

3. Examining new maize varieties at Meru in Kenya.

greatly improve the protein content and hence the nutritional value of the grains. Many of the new varieties of cereals too are quick-maturing, enabling farmers to grow several crops a year.

There is even a new man-made cereal, triticale, originating in Canada from a cross between durum wheat and rye. It was originally hoped that it could be used to extend the grain-growing zone northwards in Canada, but research has indicated that it is likely to be more useful in mountain areas of the sub-tropics, and so its development has been transferred to CIMMYT. Under certain conditions it can produce a higher yield and grain of better protein quality than either wheat or rye.

Improved Crop Husbandry

The provision of these new 'super-seeds' is only one aspect of the Green Revolution. To give the optimum results they need to be used with skill and intelligence. The farmers who sow them need to have a knowledge of the basic plant foods, namely nitrogen, potash and phosphates, and to understand how these may be supplied when the soil is deficient.

For purposes such as these, most countries now have agricultural advisory services with district officers whose duty it is to instruct farmers in the new techniques. Some are more efficient than others.

Many tropical soils are badly leached — that is, the heavy rains have washed out many of the plant nutrients they originally contained. The deficit may be made up by incorporating into the soil either organic or inorganic fertilizers. Organic fertilizers consist of plant or animal residues — in other words, compost or dung. Composting, or the breaking down of plant debris to form humus, is a technique familiar in China and parts of India and the far east, but not so well known in Africa and tropical America. It is extremely useful on a small scale, but making sufficient compost to fertilize large areas imposes formidable problems. The use of animal excreta for fertilizer is limited in much of India and in some other lands by the practice of employing it as fuel.

Applying measured quantities of balanced fertilizer is a simpler technique, widely practised in most western countries but encountering strong deterrents in much of the developing world. The chief handicap is price. Many countries have no fertilizer manufacturing industry, so all supplies have to be imported, with transport added to the initial costs. And at present not nearly enough fertilizers are being manufactured to supply the potential market.

Many farmers in the developing countries are faced with an unhappy dilemma. In order to get the increased yields of which the new varieties of seed are capable, they need to spend money on fertilizers; but then they find that the money they will get from the increase is less than the amount they have had to spend in fertilizers.

Even more unenviable was the plight of an African farmer who was persuaded to try some of the new improved maize. As a leader in his community he felt that it was up to him to set an example. So he sowed a hectare or two of the new seed, gave it the recommended treatment with fertilizer and in due course reaped the promised harvest. He was pleased and his neighbours were impressed. Next year he doubled the area sown, but in that year the rains failed to fall at the expected time. The maize wilted and died. His harvest hardly equalled the amount of seed he had sown. 'I am worse off now than I was before,' he lamented. 'Then I had nothing. Now again I have nothing, but also I owe for the seed corn and fertilizer.'

The example illustrates another basic need of plants — water. Not only are most plants composed largely of water (as are we ourselves) but they can absorb the essential plant nutrients only in solution. To apply fertilizers without the assurance that there will be sufficient water to dissolve them is a waste of resources.

Irrigation schemes are therefore of prime importance, especially in hot countries where the evaporation rate is high. Great areas of the tropical world remain unused or only partially exploited through lack of water. As it happens, considerable areas of these lands have large resources of subterranean water which may one day transform them. In the meantime most irrigation schemes are concerned with diverting river water into a network of small channels for watering fields. Many of the larger projects are designed primarily for the production of electricity, with irrigation as a secondary target.

The use of the new seeds, coupled with irrigation and the application of fertilizer, calls for a more advanced skill in crop husbandry than most peasant farmers possess. For instance, the growing of rice in flooded paddy fields is a technique familiar to many farmers in India, China and the far east, but not to those of Africa. An African farmer of the savanna zone is accustomed to having his year divided into two main sections — a dry season and a wet one. Sometimes a minor wet season, 'the little rains', subdivides the dry one. His life therefore consists of alternating periods of intense activity and leisure.

The new methods of crop husbandry require sustained effort around the calendar. The expense of the new seed, fertilizers and irrigation make it imperative that the farmer grow a succession of crops. While one rice harvest is ripening, another must be in the course of preparation in the nurseries, ready for transplanting. Even more advanced is the theory of the rotation of crops, whereby vegetables or some other crop alternates with the main cereal (rice, for example) in order to prevent the build-up of specific diseases and the exhaustion of plant nutrients. A peasant who has previously grown nothing but maize or sorghum finds all this difficult to master; and the loss of the months of leisure requires even greater powers of adaptation.

Markets

If the world is to be fed, the peasants of the developing countries must produce a surplus of food. That in itself is a novel concept to many of them. In vast regions of the third world subsistence farming is traditional. A peasant has had enough trouble producing sufficient food for his family to eat, let alone a surplus for sale. To many primitive peoples a cash economy is a novelty. The present generation is the first one ever to have had to handle money.

The attitude towards self-sufficiency is deeply ingrained. In a bustling west African city I found behind the modern bungalow of a distinguished cleric a plot of land where he was growing maize. His instinct and tradition told him that he ought to be growing at least some food for his family. Yet if the population of the rapidly-growing towns (which are a new phenomenon in Africa and to a lesser extent in many other regions) is to be fed, the food has to come from farms outside the urban limits. They must not place too much reliance on backyard farming.

On the other hand, the food-producing farms must be sufficiently near the town concerned for the cost of transport not to be prohibitive. In Central America I talked with an enterprising young farmer who was getting impressive production from his few hectares of fertile land. But he had little incentive to grow more than sufficient for his family. The nearest town large enough to offer a worthwhile market was more than a hundred miles away. The ideal juxtaposition is that illustrated by the copper belt of Zambia, where towns housing workers employed at a wage which gives them purchasing power are surrounded by a zone of small farms. These concentrate on producing eggs, poultry meat, rabbit meat, vegetables and fruit.

The production of a surplus leads on to the problems of marketing. Here the peasants encounter a problem familiar to agriculturists and indeed to primary producers of any commodity the world over. The customer wants to buy as cheaply as possible. Even in the western world money spent on food is often begrudged. The tendency is always to economize on essentials in order to leave more cash to spare for luxuries.

In another Central American country members of a tribe of jungle Indians told me how much they disliked taking their surplus produce to the nearest market — an excursion involving a day's journey by canoe. They complained, 'The traders see us coming, and they know we come from a long way and can't afford to take our goods back. So they offer us the lowest prices possible, and we have to take them.'

I have also met the problem of the peasants who, having doubled their production by using new seeds and new techniques, have found that the price of their products has halved, leaving them no better off than before. The natural inclination of peasant farmers who have had such experiences is to restrict production. Why make the extra effort if there are no rewards?

One solution to the difficulty is offered by co-operative marketing. Co-operatives of all kinds have sprung up like mushrooms in the developing countries, and many of them have disintegrated just as quickly. There have been co-operatives for the purchase or use of farm machinery, co-operatives for irrigation projects, co-operatives for the development of new areas of land, and dozens of others, but many of the most successful have been concerned with marketing.

One of the things which co-operatives, or on a larger scale government agencies, have to do is to provide storage space for crops, so that they can be released to the market in an orderly manner. The huge increases in yields produced by the new seeds and new techniques caught more than one country unawares. The farmers who employed the new methods were, in so many instances, so obviously successful that their neighbours wanted to follow their example. This, of course, is exactly what was wanted, but the speed and extent of the revolution was overwhelming. In West Pakistan, after the new rice IR-8 had proved its worth, in one year (1967–68) the acreage of land growing rice increased from 10,000 to nearly 1 million! There were not the storage, drying, transport and marketing facilities to cope with such a prodigious expansion.

Such problems, inherent in success, can of course be overcome, given time. More fundamental ones, however, are dealt with in the next chapter.

3

HINDRANCES

Money and Expertise

The basic problem of feeding a world population expanding at a phenomenal rate, formidable though it is, is overshadowed by one of equal urgency. Perhaps it is best to regard the two as one complex whole.

We have seen that the implementation of the Green Revolution demands a fairly high degree of skill and expertise, as well as adequate financial resources. These demands are being made to a primarily peasant population, many of whom are at a quite primitive state of culture. Can they hope to meet them?

There are still people who gain their living by hunting, even in thickly populated regions such as west Africa. There are many others who are nomadic, following their herds on seasonal migrations. The abattoirs of Kenya and other countries of tropical Africa get enormous numbers of cattle from such tribes who wander down from the savanna country on the margins of the Sahara, allowing their animals to feed on the seasonal grass as they move southwards. Leaving aside these peoples for the moment, it is true to say that the great mass of the population of the third world consists of peasant farmers.

Certain tribes in Zambia (where there is still plenty of space) are at an interesting transitional stage, which may be termed semi-nomadic — though at the time of my last visit official attempts were being made to move them through it quickly.

4. Still at the hunting stage in Nigeria.

A tribe, roaming through the bush, lights upon a spot which seems attractive for a temporary settlement. There is water nearby, and the soil (to judge from the luxuriance of the bush) is reasonably fertile. So the tribe builds itself a village of wattle and thatch huts in a clearing and sets about preparing plots for cultivation. This they do by the slash-and-burn technique. With their machetes, or pangas, they attack a defined area of bush, hacking down all the smaller bushes that are within their capacity and even managing to fell some of the lesser trees. Around the larger trees and around fallen trunks they pile brushwood and set fire to it. Sometimes, inevitably, the fire gets out of control, but no matter; it simply makes a greater area of land available for planting.

Just as the rains are starting they plant the land with maize (or sorghum or some similar cereal), setting each seed separately into a hole in the soil made by a pointed stick. There is no attempt at planting the seed in rows, nor can there be, for the whole plot is littered with ash-blackened tree branches and jagged stumps.

In due course the harvest is reaped by slashing down the maize stalks with the same pangas and, after the removal of the cobs, burning the straw. Thus the basic or cereal part of its diet is provided for, while the tribe obtains the rest of its food by hunting and fishing.

After the tribe has cultivated the land in this fashion for several years, diminishing crop yields indicate that the fertility of the soil is declining. It is time to move on. So the village is abandoned and the tribe departs, leaving the bush to reclaim its traditional territory.

This slash-and-burn system of farming is still common among some tribes of the tropics. It naturally operates most successfully where there is ample space for the tribe to be nomadic. Where the tribe is restricted to a permanent settlement, the system is modified by attempting to farm the land within reach on a rota basis. A general rule is that one can return to an abandoned plot after about eight years – though as a region has become more thickly populated the period has in some instances been reduced to as low as four years. During the interval, whatever it is, the soil has had a chance to replenish some of its fertility and yet the bush has not grown too formidable to be tackled by machetes.

Visiting the Valiente Indians of north-eastern Panama I found that they were bound by a tradition which imposed a fifteen-year gap before land could be used again. The rule had evidently been worked out in past ages when the tribe had plenty of jungle-space, but now they were cooped up in a permanent village on a narrow, rugged peninsula. They were forced to go farther and farther from base to find land which their traditions told them they could legitimately use for crops. But tradition was so strong that they would undertake a two-hour marathon tramp along crazy mountain and jungle trails to reach their small fields rather than try to break with convention.

Where bush or jungle is the natural vegetation, the slash-and-burn routine is technically sound. It approximates to the fallow period characteristic of crop rotations in western countries. After a period of utilization the soil is given a time of rest, in order to renew its fertility. The ash from the burnt vegetation does, in addition, add a little to the resources of the soil.

In many tropical countries settlement has reached a further stage. Much of rural Africa is netted with roads and tracks linking villages which, to the uninitiated eye, are almost indistinguishable from each other. In the villages live small farmers each of whom has a house, or a group of huts, and sufficient land (in theory) on which to grow food for his family. His plots of land are not usually contiguous but are scattered about in the village territory. The settlement itself is engulfed in a vast wilderness which, forbidding though it may appear, is not technically waste. It belongs either to the tribe as a whole or to some of its members. Even what appears to be unreclaimed jungle may be a part of somebody's private holding, and there are also grazing rights, charcoal-burning rights and other claims to be taken into account.

Lacking (until recently) a cash economy, and in any case engaged in solely subsistence farming, such village communities are, until hit by the impact of the modern world, held together by rigid custom based on a patriarchal or tribal system. Under this system each member has his obligations and rights, much as under the old feudal system in Europe. If a group of European peasants of, say, the seventh to twelfth centuries AD could come face to face with their counterparts in much of present-day Africa, Asia or Latin America, all parties would find themselves on recognizable common ground.

Although the ratio is changing, as the new towns of the third world grow at an explosive rate, 70% to 90% of the population in most of the developing countries are still peasants. It is they who must carry the burden of feeding the proliferating population. And they are being asked to make in one or two generations progress which took European peasants a thousand years. The wonder is not that they have so much further to go but that they have already achieved so much.

But let us look more closely at some of the mental attitudes which, more than anything else, are the chief obstacles to success.

In southern India I was asked to advise about a crop of rice that was turning yellow in the four-leaf stage.

'It looks like nitrogen deficiency to me,' I suggested. 'Do you have any information about the field?'

'Oh yes. We've had the soil analysed.'

They produced the soil analysis chart. Sure enough, it said, 'Nitrogen: very deficient.'

'But didn't I see some bags of fertilizer in the store?'

We returned to the store, and there they were — bags containing half a ton of nitrogenous fertilizer.

These farmers had all the information they needed about the impending failure of their rice crop. They had at hand the means to correct the deficiency and save the crop. But because no one had told them what to do, they were allowing the fertilizer to stay in the store and the crop to wilt.

In another Indian village a group of farmers were digging a well. It was their fourth attempt. The other three had ended in failure because at a certain depth the well had caved in. The diggers had struck a pocket of soft substratum which made it imperative that they should line the well.

But the lesson had not been learnt. Wells were dug in a certain way, and they had followed the conventional rules. It was just bad luck, or the will of an inscrutable Providence, that had caused their efforts to fail. Instead of moving to a new site, or taking steps to line the well, they were repeating the operation exactly as before, hoping that this time God would be kinder to them.

Cattle and other livestock are a symbol of wealth in many rural societies in the third world. They are valued for the status they bring, not for any qualities of their own. They are also currency — so many cows to purchase a wife.

Again, in southern India I visited a farm which was being managed quite well, as far as the crops were concerned. The manager evidently understood arable farming. But the farm animals were another matter entirely. He took me to see his pigs. About twenty of them, all sizes, were running together in a small enclosure. They were much like the under-sized runts depicted scavenging on rubbish heaps in medieval paintings in Europe.

'A sow farrowed last week,' the manager told me.

'How many in the litter?'

'Oh, only two. And one died.'

But, to crown it all, about a fortnight before my visit the headman of the village asked for a pig for a feast. Naturally he got it. Naturally, as it was an important feast, they killed the biggest pig in the herd. The only full-grown boar!

The persons involved in these three stories were literate. They had had an education of sorts. In that respect they were a stage ahead of most of the peasants of the developing countries. It is a sobering thought that in this sophisticated and technically progressive century there are more illiterates in the world than ever before. On what can an illiterate person rely for guidelines through his difficult life? He is at the mercy of what he is told. And what he is told consists largely of the inherited traditions of his people, incorporating a medley of superstitions and religious beliefs.

Superstition

One of the common features of nearly all primitive traditions is the provision of alibis. Life is so hard that clearly no man could accept the burden of responsibility for the misfortunes that are heaped upon him. What causes famines? The failure of the rains. Can a man do anything about that? No, it is the will of God.

Illness and death are not natural events, subject to the laws of cause and effect. They are due to the capricious pranks of higher powers or, more probably, to witchcraft. The desire to blame someone for disaster is universal. We know well enough that, when a road accident occurs in our own country, of twenty spectators perhaps three will be found helping the injured while the other seventeen stand around discussing whose fault it was.

When a bus, built to carry 40 passengers but loaded with 150, careering along a dusty road from the inland west African country of Upper Volta on its way to the coast, hits a sheep at 50 m.p.h. and charges into a ditch, the driver escapes unscathed. The survivors later swear that when they were crawling from the wreckage they saw him approaching on foot from a point fifty yards away. This they ascribe not to his agility in seeing what was about to happen and jumping clear, but to the fact that he wore a powerful amulet around his neck. This amulet magically whisked him out of the vehicle and deposited him in a safe place just before the impact. He had a good ju-ju.

Spells, ju-jus, fetishes and talismans are agents to ward off mishaps and bad luck. Certainly that there is any connexion between food and hygiene on the one hand and health on the other is a novel and unacceptable concept. When the idea is first brought to their notice they will have none of it. It would put too much responsibility on their own shoulders.

I called at an Indian village just after a little girl had died. The customary wailing and mourning were in full spate. The child, it was said, had been

5. Starving children at a clinic in Dahomey, west Africa.

playing happily on the previous day and had suddenly been taken ill. It was a worm. It had come up into her throat and choked her. Someone professed to have seen it.

The doctor insisted on conducting a post-mortem. It was revealed that the little girl had had pleurisy. The illness could not have been as sudden as the family said. She must have been ill for days, and her death was in fact partly attributable to neglect. Her family and friends did not want to hear that sort of talk, not on any account. She had always been, they said, a 'poor doer'. It was the will of God that she should be taken from them, and they wished to mourn her passing in the accepted fashion, without any uneasy suggestions that fault might lie with them.

Throughout the tropics I came across innumerable examples of ill-health and death being attributed to witchcraft. How much more satisfying to blame some malignant person than to swallow such far-fetched tales as illness being due to drinking water from the hole where the buffaloes wallow; or, even more fantastic, to disease being carried by harmless little nuisances such as flies buzzing into the kitchen from the adjacent latrine.

Besides, diseases are to be expected. Some debilitating maladies are so widespread that the sufferers are unaware that they are ill. They think that their familiar state of lethargy and discomfort is natural.

Gordon Rattray Taylor estimates that 70% of the people of lower Egypt are suffering from schistosomiasis or bilharzia, the wasting disease carried by water-snails. As a result the life expectancy there of men is 25 years, of women 27. Bilharzia is now, he says, the world's most widespread disease, afflicting an estimated 114 million people. Add to those the victims (now increasing in numbers) of malaria, sleeping sickness and the numerous fevers and infections that harass dwellers in tropical lands, and the realization grows that a large proportion of the peasants of the third world live in a state of chronic ill-health. It is no wonder that many of them jib at the idea of altering their ancient farming systems to one which will require that they work more hours under the blistering sun. Many of them are not capable of more than a few hours of work per day. Illiterate, under-nourished, ravaged by disease, these under-privileged members of the human race are those placed in the forefront of the battle for survival. It is not surprising that production so often lags far behind the potential.

Education – 1

The natural reaction of many an intelligent boy faced with such an overwhelming challenge and with everything apparently against him is to run away from it. For his people for untold generations life on the land has meant drudgery with a hoe. His over-riding ambition is to get away. Within the present century he has found what he supposes is a path of escape. It is called Education.

Europeans have been largely responsible for the near disastrous attitudes towards education that have developed in much of the third world. They could hardly be blamed for taking their western standards of living with them when they went to live in the tropical world, but their way of life was certainly a revelation to many of the people among whom they settled.

The villagers took note. These newcomers, whether there as administrators, traders, mine supervisors or missionaries, occupied weatherproof bungalows that were better than a chief's hut. They had three adequate meals a day, reclined on comfortable furniture, possessed the amenities of paraffin lighting (followed later by electricity), a telephone and a bathroom. They travelled in a car or some other sort of vehicle; certainly they seldom walked. They employed servants to do all the menial tasks about the compound. And, as far as the villagers understood work, they did no work at all. They talked, or they sat on their backsides at desks.

All this, to the peasant of the third world, represented and still represents a very desirable state of affairs. Having considered the situation deeply, he concludes that the key to this paradise is education. Once a man is educated, he too can sit in an office and give orders to his inferiors. A peasant family will therefore make sustained sacrifices to get at least a few members educated.

The Extended Family

We must digress a little to give some consideration to the extended family of the third world, otherwise no proper understanding of the problems of the developing countries can be achieved. It is particularly common and dominant in Africa. Near the town of Wa, in northern Ghana, I was invited into a house typical of that part of inland west Africa. It was built of baked mud, single-storeyed and with a low, flat roof. From the road one saw a covered veranda with a mud bench on which a middle-aged woman sat, offering for sale measures of meal. Children played around her, younger women scuttled in and out of the house, and an old grandfather lolled in the shade, smoking his pipe and watching passers-by. Peeping through the gateway into the courtyard I could see great earthenware jars bubbling over an open fire.

The interior came as a revelation. Here was not so much a house as an entire village, grouped around a series of inner courtyards. I was accustomed to seeing the open-plan arrangement common in countries of east Africa, where a house consists of a number of single-roomed huts around an open space, but this was a labyrinth of connected passages and buildings. Some were open-sided sheds, others rooms of which only a glimpse could be obtained through dark doorways. In one yard a spreading mango tree gave shade to another grandfather who was playing with a naked baby kicking on a rug; in another, three men sat sipping palm wine, a brew made in the cauldrons over the fire. Other buildings were devoted to the refining of shea butter, of which large pans were set out to cool.

In all, the compound could not have occupied less than half an acre and probably spread over a considerably wider area. The whole was enclosed within a fortress-like mud wall.

As for the residents, I saw at least forty. As with rabbits, those visible were probably only a minor proportion of those actually present. They represented, in concentrated form, the African extended family. All were related. Here were fathers, mothers, children, uncles, aunts, cousins of various degrees, grandparents and quite probably polygamous wives whose children further complicated relationships.

6. A household courtyard in northern Ghana.

To find a whole family, or a large part of it, under one roof or in one compound is quite common right round the tropics, from Melanesia to Central America. In such societies an individual counts for less and family loyalty for more than we in the west are accustomed. A man's relevance lies in his membership of a family.

Sometimes this gives rise to what we would consider unusual arrangements, as for example when a man inherits not from his father but from his uncle. The son of a wealthy man may even find himself penniless on his father's death (and, indeed, in the bad old days instances occurred of uncles selling their orphaned nephews and nieces into slavery); but the traditions ensure that the money and other property remain in the family.

The extended family is a group for mutual protection in a potentially hostile world. As long as a man sticks to his family, and it is unthinkable that he should not, he has a measure of security. When there is food he will have his share, even if he is old, incapacitated or sick. Similarly, if he is doing well he is expected to share his prosperity with his family.

I saw the beneficent side of the extended family in the east central province of Nigeria (the one-time Biafra) after the civil war. On visiting it to see how recovery and rehabilitation were progressing, I was surprised by how few orphans were in institutional homes. All but a few had been absorbed into families. One African church minister with eight children of his own had adopted four more. That is the extended family at its best.

A new mission hospital in the Ivory Coast had only two doctors and an endless queue of patients.

'What do the people down in the town think of having this splendid hospital on their doorstep?' I asked.

'I'm afraid they regard us as a bit of a curse!'

'Why?' I asked, startled.

'Patients come, you see, from as much as a hundred miles away. They walk here, with all their families, and descend on their relations in the town. It is taken for granted that they will be given food and hospitality for as long as they need it. And sometimes they have to wait for a month or two before we can deal with them.'

Also in the Ivory Coast I met a young teacher who had just been visited by his brother. His uncle had recently died back at home in Mali several hundreds of miles away, and the young man's father had sent a brother down to collect from the teacher £40 towards funeral expenses. There was no question of enquiring whether the teacher could afford it. The father was head of the house; he had every right to make the demand. The teacher did not have £40, so he borrowed it.

In another instance, when a young farmer secured a loan for agricultural improvements on his land, three uncles demanded shares of it. By the time he had doled out what they asked for, there was precious little left for him to use in taking his part in the Green Revolution. And this was not a grant but a loan which, theoretically at any rate, had to be repaid by the young man if not by the uncles.

The extended family will make great sacrifices to enable some of its youngsters to have an education. I have heard many bitter complaints that once a boy was educated he was of no use on the farm. They were justified. Most of them came from Europeans. Africans understood the situation perfectly. Of course he was of no use on the farm. The whole idea behind having him educated was to enable him to get away from it. To return to the old drudgery would have been a negation of everything he and they had worked for.

Moreover, the educated boy needs to use his education to acquire some cash. He has to pay back the money advanced, so that the next bright boy of the family may go to school. That applies even when a boy is given a technical agricultural education.

In a west African country I talked with two young men who were in their final term of a three-year course at an agricultural college. The government of this country was taking an enlightened attitude towards education. It appreciated that the schools and colleges were turning out boys and girls for whom no jobs were available, so it had taken steps to ensure that reasonable alternatives were provided for those who had to return to the villages. Before boys were accepted for the practical and comprehensive agricultural course at this college they had to sign a document stating that, on its completion, they would take up farming on their own account. Their fathers and the chief of their village also signed a declaration that land would be available for them and that every facility and encouragement would be given for them to establish themselves as modern, enlightened farmers.

As watertight a scheme as could be devised, one would say. So I spoke with these two young men:

'You will be going back to farm in your village?'

'Oh yes, sir.'

'And putting into practice all you have been learning?'

'Oh yes, sir.'

'But not just yet,' one of them added.

'Why not?'

'Well, you see, first we have to get jobs to earn money, so that we can repay our families for our education.'

The familiar snare. Down to the coast they would go, seeking for probably non-existent jobs. Both they and their families would be in one mind about that. Would they ever come back?

If they were lucky enough to find good posts in the city, they must never think that their good fortune and the attendant salary were their own affair — nor would they. They would know that they were expected to share everything with the family which had piloted them to their exalted positions. The bigger the salary, the greater the number of relations who would arrive to share it with them.

The African extended family explains many of the things that happen in African politics. What we in the west might consider nepotism and corruption is, from an African point of view, merely a man looking after his family in the manner expected of him.

Churches are, of course, by no means exempt from the general involvement in family life. African clergy, like all the other reasonably affluent Africans, find themselves supporting as many members of the extended family as is commensurate with their stipend — usually more. They seldom have enough to go round. Therefore most clergy, together with most other educated Africans in other walks of life, have their own little farms and often a shop as well. They need them all.

However, it is very difficult for an African to accumulate enough capital to run his farm by modern methods, even if he knows what they are. He has too many hangers-on.

Education — 2

Let us return from our examination of the extended family to look more closely at the system of education to which these youngsters are subjected. Their catastrophically mistaken attitude towards it is very largely due to the errors of the first schools. The early educationalists, many of them missionaries with the best intentions, transplanted a European system into alien soil. The first generation of scholars learned Latin, European history, European geography, European law and similar abstruse subjects which bore no relationship to their daily life. Even the examples they found in their mathematical textbooks were European. The problems spoke of apples, jam and other commodities to youngsters who had never seen such things. It bade them calculate in miles, acres, gallons and other measurements which were completely foreign.

In the early 1970s a teacher told me she found that her east African pupils could recite the rivers of Europe but could not even name the great river which flowed six miles away.

'What is a hill?' she once asked.

'A hill is an eminence of less elevation than a mountain,' the class chorused.

She took them outside and pointed to the horizon.

'There, that is a hill.'

They looked at her with eyes round with wonder. They had never before realized that what they had been learning from books bore any relationship to what they could see around them.

Because what they learned at school seemed to have so little relevance to their daily life, generations of students came to regard education as contained in a watertight compartment. Education was the key to the way of escape to a better life. It was nothing more. One learnt all those facts about remote places and events for one purpose only, and that was to pass the examination which produced the coveted diploma, degree or certificate. Armed with that, one was entitled to a white-collar job which gave one a seat at a desk and authority to give orders to less qualified persons.

So widespread and deep-rooted became this attitude that it was applied to all subjects taught in schools. Wise agricultural officials in a west African country assured me that once agriculture was taught as a subject in a school, with an examination at the end of the course, the students would be lost for ever to any practical work on farms. 'They will have passed an examination,' they said, 'which they think should entitle them to something better.'

Education European-style was all very well as long as only the top 5% of the population were being educated. From that élite the present generation of administrators, politicians, lawyers, businessmen and clergy came, and very able some of them are. So too is the next generation. There are among them many clever, lively, ambitious young men and women who clamour for the places they consider to be rightfully theirs.

The problem arises from their greater numbers. In many countries, especially in Africa, perhaps 60% or 70% of children and adolescents attend some sort of school. Almost all go with the fixed intention of obtaining the certificate, diploma, degree or other scrap of paper which will be their passport to a life as far away from the land as possible. Yet in most of the countries concerned the economy is still based 80% or 90% on agriculture and is likely to be until at least the end of the century.

If ever there were a recipe for disaster, this is it.

The politicians know this and are at their wits' end to discover what to do about it. Each year a new crop of intelligent school-leavers makes for the

7. A *favela* in Rio de Janeiro, Brazil.

nearest big town if they are not already there, and begins the heart-breaking search for non-existent jobs. (Kenya, one of the more progressive and prosperous of African nations, recently had less than a million people in paid jobs, out of a population of over 10 million.) Perhaps one youngster in twenty finds a berth — just enough to encourage next year's contingent to tread the same path. Those back at home hear of the successful one but not of the nineteen who drift frustrated into unemployment in the slums, the *favelas* of the South American cities. There they meet with others in the same cul-de-sac and, fed up and disillusioned, are readier than most to hatch a revolution.

Some governments have taken the drastic steps of rounding up unemployed young dissidents from time to time and carting them back to their native villages. But there is little to stop them from drifting back again. For the fact is that young men – and women – will never willingly stay on the land and live in villages until by so doing they can enjoy a standard of living at least equal to that of their brothers who go to the towns and manage to find jobs. In west Africa I learned that a youth who went down to one of the ports and secured a job as a dock labourer for two months out of twelve, remaining unemployed for the rest of the year, was still financially better off than his brother who stayed at home working hard on the farm.

There are of course other factors than the purely financial involved. Life in a bush village, without electricity, piped water and almost every other amenity, can be exceedingly dull. The gay lights and noisy juke-boxes of the city have their attractions. Yet money is at the root of the problem. If money were available, a village youth with cash in his pocket could afford occasional visits to the town. He could buy transistor radios or bicycles or nylon shirts. But how much money can he expect to receive from a family farm of a few hectares, already supporting his father and umpteen members of the extended family? The answer is, of course, none.

The Dilemma

Here then is the dilemma of the developing nations. With populations increasing at astronomical rates, they urgently need increased levels of food production to provide for them. Yet they are breeding generations of young people desperately eager to have nothing to do with the soil.

In Europe too we are familiar with the mentality, widely prevalent until a few decades ago, that the educated townsman was superior to the bucolic countryman. Even in advanced countries such as Switzerland there was until recently a distinct difference in the standards of life of the city-dweller and the villager. In the third world the contrasts are more pronounced, and everyone there knows it.

The principal of an excellent farm project in Sri Lanka told me, 'The problem of our young men here is to find educated wives. Girls with an education can do better than marry farmers.'

A central African village chieftain commented, 'What's the use of sending boys to school? There are no jobs for them when they leave.'

No office jobs, that is. Agricultural work doesn't count. You can go farming without an education.

So the most important and urgent task in the world today is despised as being unworthy of an intelligent young man. It is the failures who go back to the hoe and the mattock, back to the endless struggle with drought and weevils, with quelea birds, locusts and rats.

What is needed, of course, is a new appreciation of the dignity of work with one's hands, and more particularly of the sanctity of labour which involves co-operation with the good earth in producing bread. It is a noble aspiration, but one which needs to be firmly rooted in realities. And the prime reality is that it is exceedingly difficult for a developing country to build up a prosperous agriculture. The reason is that the hungry section of the populace for whom the farmer is required to produce food consists of just those citizens who have no money to pay for it.

How ways of escape are being sought from this dilemma and what hope there is of eventual salvation is discussed in the final chapter.

4

THE HELPERS

To dispel to some extent any feeling of fatalism and hopelessness which may have been invoked by the preceding chapter, let us look at some of the positive steps being taken to improve food production and rural life, and at some of the agencies involved.

In the first place, almost every emergent nation has its ministry of agriculture. Most of these ministries operate an advisory service, involving a network of advisory officers each with his own territory. Some of them have gone so far as to create a superfluity of advisory officers, as for example an African state which has cotton-growing advisory officers in areas where no cotton is grown! In theory, at least, every peasant farmer has access to an official who should be able to give him expert advice on whatever his technical problems may be.

The advisory service is, in most countries, backed by a chain of experimental stations, research centres, agricultural colleges and university departments, to which the officers may turn with any problem on which they feel they need further information. In some of these establishments courses are available for farmers, and it is part of the advisory officers' job to recruit farmers for them.

On paper the organization is excellent, but its efficiency depends on two things. One is the quality of its servants; the other, the availability of the necessary money. The quality of the servants is variable — some are splendid, devoted men, while some may be described as parasites. The money is often non-existent.

In practice, too, the officers and the centres from which they work are too few for the task. There is thus ample scope for organizations from other countries to take a share in the work.

51

The Churches

At the grass-roots level many of these external agencies are associated with the churches. That is a natural development from the period when missionaries established the first schools and were for a time responsible for providing the only formal education available. In most countries (though there are some exceptions, such as Belize) the government has taken over control of the schools from the churches, but specialist colleges, such as those for agriculture, often remain in church hands. Relations between church and state are usually excellent, for the governments appreciate that they are faced with a bigger task than they can comfortably cope with and so welcome any allies.

The type of agricultural work in which the churches find themselves involved varies considerably. As this was an aspect of rural development in the third world with which I was closely involved for five years, I shall give a few examples.

In Kenya the church with which I was serving was running a fine little agricultural college in the uplands near Mount Kenya, bringing in farmers for short courses and sending out extension officers to follow up their pupils and help them on their own farms. It worked closely with government officials engaged in much the same work. Down on the lower Tana river other smaller schemes, based on irrigation, were developing. Other churches had their own projects, some of them very similar. In the Masai country one had pioneered with the idea of persuading the tribesmen to break with the old tradition of communal grazing. Any family which was willing to do so was allowed to enclose up to 2,000 acres of land and to take its share of cattle, often amounting to 200 or 300, from the communal herds, while at the same time it could apply for government grants for water supplies and fencing. The Masai were just beginning to realize that a family with 2,000 acres of land and 200 to 300 head of cattle was wealthy in any country. As they have always regarded themselves as an aristocracy among the neighbours, the concept has appealed to them. Whether it will prove a wise development in the long run remains to be seen.

In Zambia also there were agricultural colleges, one of the most important taking in students for a course lasting several years. Some of the old mission schools also had farms attached, and individual missionaries were engaged in agricultural work in villages, such as the organization of cooperatives.

Rhodesia presented a dilemma. Here the churches had inherited, largely by gift, huge areas of land. These were settled by African farmers, whom

8. Masai herdsmen in Kenya.

the churches were trying to help to become more efficient. However, the churches were basically in the position of landlords, a role which they did not like but which they could not escape, for as long as they remained they acted as a kind of buffer between their tenants and the Smith régime which controlled the country. If they tried to co-operate with the illegal government, they reaped ill-will in some quarters; if they did not, they created enemies in others. Nevertheless with these handicaps they still struggled to do a worthwhile job.

In west Africa I found diverse agricultural projects run by the churches in Nigeria, Dahomey (now Benin), Togo, Ghana, Ivory Coast, Sierra Leone and the Gambia. The Honda training scheme already described (see page 24) was based on a small reclamation project in Sierra Leone which was doing excellent work in the promotion of the growing of upland rice, a development which the government was doing its utmost to foster. The Dahomey project was catering for village boys who had no other opportunity for education. Nigeria had a demonstration farm with a poultry co-operative attached.

In India the churches possessed large compounds attached to hospitals, schools and other properties, which it would have been shameful to leave uncultivated in that land of hunger. Farms ranging from about an acre to

53

200 or 300 acres were operating, at varying levels of efficiency. Some had been the recipients of first-class farm livestock and machinery, organized by charitable bodies in Europe. Some were successfully demonstrating modern methods of husbandry; others were not.

In the western hemisphere the chief agricultural work in which I became involved was in Haiti, a poverty-stricken land in which almost any change was bound to be for the better. Several multi-purpose projects were in progress, one of which is described in more detail in our final chapter.

Other Agencies

Valuable as all the work thus surveyed undoubtedly was, it was but a drop in the ocean compared with the need. In each of the countries concerned, too, the work of the church which I served was paralleled by that of other churches and by many charitable organizations. Christian Aid and Oxfam, for instance, operate in a wider range of countries than any of the British churches. The Americans are active on an even larger scale. Their church overseas operations are co-ordinated by a high-powered organization, Church World Service, with imposing headquarters in New York. Other western countries — notably West Germany, the Netherlands, France, Norway and Switzerland — likewise have efficient Christian organizations in the field. Some countries allocate a proportion of their taxes to the development of the third world, channelling the funds through the voluntary agencies.

Higher on the political scale several countries, including the United Kingdom, have ministries of overseas development, with considerable budgets. Much of their work consists in diverting technical aid and skilled personnel to those countries which ask for them.

In our consideration of the Green Revolution we took note of a number of important international organizations which support the research centres from which the new seeds emanate. The two banks mentioned, the World Bank and the Inter-American Development Bank, serve to remind us that banks are international and exist to lend money to profitable enterprises. In Africa I was able to initiate several worthwhile schemes by introducing them to local banks. The Ford Foundation and the Rockefeller Foundation are examples of the way in which great commercial empires can use some of their resources philanthropically.

The supreme international organization, however, is of course the United Nations. Under its spacious roof it houses a whole family of organizations dedicated to improving the standard of life in its member countries.

One with particular relevance in the campaign to improve the prospects of the third world is the United Nations Conference on Trade and Development (UNCTAD), established in 1964 to

promote international trade, especially with a view to accelerating economic development, particularly trade between countries at different stages of development, between developing countries and between countries with different systems of economic and social organization . . .

Another is the United Nations Development Programme (UNDP), the aim of which is to

help low-income nations build productive, dynamic societies and economies based on the full effective use of their own natural and human resources . . . the Programme supports projects, requested by the governments of low-income countries, which are designed to help these nations attract the development capital, train the skilled manpower, and apply the modern technologies needed to improve and expand agriculture, industry, transport, communications, educational systems and medical and social services.

Among other international bodies are the International Organization for Rural Development, and the Afro-Asian Rural Reconstruction Organization. The latter, with headquarters in New Delhi, aims

to develop understanding among members for better appreciation of each other's problems and to explore collectively opportunities for the co-ordination of efforts for promoting welfare and eradication of hunger and poverty amongst rural people in Africa and Asia.

The Food and Agricultural Organization of the United Nations (FAO) has multifarious activities in many countries. Some of its projects have far-reaching implications. At Lanet in Kenya I inspected a cattle-fattening enterprise roughly on the lines of an American beef feedlot. Batches of lean cattle were brought in and programme-fed on balanced rations. The process extended over about sixty days. To the surprise and gratification of many interested agriculturists, on certain rations the native cattle — lean, Zebu-humped animals — put on flesh faster and more economically than did those of European breeds. The door seems to be opening for the development of a large-scale beef production industry in east Africa.

One of the problems is that of finding the food for the cattle. That is one of the difficulties of keeping livestock in the tropics. Most of the countries concerned are so short of food that they need it all for the human population. In this instance, the problem was solved by attaching sufficient land to the experimental station for the project to grow its own. Poultry-farmers endeavouring to introduce mass-production methods into sundry third

9. Cattle in a feedlot at Lanet in Kenya.

world countries encounter the same difficulty and often seek to solve it in the same way.

Another promising development in which scientists of many lands are involved is the use of African wild game for food. Experiments have shown that, by more efficient grazing habits, the wild animals of Africa can produce more food from a given area than can European-type cattle.

Some governments have ministries or special departments devoted to rural development, as in Uganda where there is a Department of Rural Economy and Extension, based on Makerere University, in Kampala. Many universities have experimental and demonstration farms, often supported to some extent by funds from overseas. The authorities in the developing countries, when offered help in rural development from a donor nation, as often as not choose a prestigious show farm, equipped with every modern aid available. In a small west African country, when I asked the Swiss director controlling such a show farm what impact his establishment had on the peasants in the surrounding district he gave me a straight answer, probably because he was leaving in the following week:

'Not the slightest,' he admitted. 'If this project were to close down now, life would go on in the villages the same as it always has, without even the smallest change through our having been here for the past four years.'

That I could well believe, for I had been visiting some of the peasants and had not been able to find even one who had set foot on the farm. (But see page 28 for a different point of view.)

Moving to the other extreme, a great deal of fundamental work has been done by the young people of the western world who have been sent out by the Voluntary Service Overseas organization and the Peace Corps to live with third world peasants. They give two years or so of their lives to social service in needy lands, working without pay and sharing as far as possible the lives of the people whom they are trying to help.

Their efforts are most successful when they work with existing and ongoing establishments. In the early days one of the mistakes frequently made was to send two or three enthusiastic youngsters into a remote district for their two years of service and then to withdraw them without replacements. Two years is certainly not long enough to achieve worthwhile results. An inexperienced young person requires much of that time to get to know the people, the language and something of the culture and traditions from which improvements have to stem. The tropics are littered with the debris of well-intentioned but ill-conceived schemes that foundered. (But see page 24 for an example of a talented Peace Corps worker co-operating with a resident missionary.)

Many of the church missions too are handicapped by frequent changes of policies and personnel. Some have a system of moving around their ministers every few years. With others, promising young men who are doing effective work have to return to their homeland in mid-career for the education of their children. In this respect the Roman Catholic Church, with a celibate priesthood, has a strong advantage. A Catholic priest will live his life through with his flock and die among them. Men who gain their living from the land change their ideas slowly. They take time to get to know and give their confidence to those who come to live in their villages. Above all, they value continuity. Even an indifferent project that staggers on, correcting its faults as it goes, is far better than one brilliantly conceived which after a few years collapses.

It must not be thought that all aid comes from the west or from Christian organizations. The communist world is almost equally active. Communist countries too provide experimental farms and rural projects, supply money for various developments, and second teachers, scientists and other personnel to work in the emerging nations. In Africa I frequently met Czech, Russian, Polish and East German workers. Chinese were also very active in such countries as Tanzania and Dahomey. It was always diplomatic to enquire of the Chinese where their allegiance lay, for some came from mainland China and some from Taiwan. Japanese businessmen, technicians and salesmen were ubiquitous.

Trade

In virtually every instance, the aid given by external bodies to the developing nations is designed to help them to be self-supporting. Relief food and free gifts are now regarded only as stop-gaps, to help to see a country through a bad patch occasioned by flood, drought, hurricane, volcanic eruption or some other natural disaster. A country must be assisted to stand on its own feet.

That implies trade; hence any survey of rural development must take account of the trading position of the countries concerned. In this respect, there has been a remarkable change of fortune for some countries during the past two decades. From being apparently hopelessly impoverished some of them have taken their place among the world's richest states. These, of course, are the oil-producing countries. Kuwait, Abu Dhabi, Dubai, Bahrein, Libya and Saudi Arabia are examples of countries which have leaped from poverty to riches almost overnight. It is to their credit that many of them have been using their new-found wealth to increase agricultural production. Old irrigation works have been restored, and new oases have suddenly appeared in the desert. Some of them have also been generous to their poorer neighbours.

Apart from oil, there has been an upsurge in the prices of certain other commodities in world markets. Primary producers have always been at the disadvantage that the whole fabric of society has been built on their shoulders. Once primary products — such as ores, fibres and foods — increase in price, the cost of everything else goes up in sympathy. Hence there has always been pressure to keep down the prices of these essential commodities, and it has been the misfortune of the third world that they are the very products on which it has had to rely.

Time and again I have heard from African farmers the sad comment that such and such a crop would not be worth growing 'if we had to pay labour, but of course we don't'. All the members of the family, including women and children, buckle to and do the necessary work, just for subsistence. To some degree, the prosperity of the advanced countries of the west has been constructed on the backs of the impoverished workers of the third world. It may justifiably be argued that, for all our vaunted aid to under-developed countries, it is really they who have been subsidizing us.

However, it is not only the oil states which have recently been enjoying a

58

10. An opencast copper mine in Zambia.

11. Sifting ground-nuts in Zambia.

change of fortunes. Minerals such as copper have been in strong demand. Jamaica began to enjoy increased prosperity when her huge bauxite deposits were exploited. Latterly too even agricultural produce has been affected. In the middle 1970s the price of ground-nuts, one of the prime products of west African countries such as Nigeria and the Gambia, suddenly quadrupled as the world became worried about protein supplies. Timber has become very expensive, a fact which has caused a number of tropical countries, including the Ivory Coast and Indonesia, to eat into their timber reserves at a rate which they may later regret.

When the EEC got itself thoroughly organized, and especially when the United Kingdom joined in, there was much anxiety among third world nations which had up to that time enjoyed a special relationship with Britain and a privileged place in her markets. In particular the sugar-producing countries were worried lest the encouragement of increased sugar-beet production in Europe should harm their traditional income from the sugar-cane harvest. As it happened, they need not have been anxious; the world market has been able to absorb all the sugar that can be produced, and at prices that give a better return to producers than formerly.

In spite of increased prices for their products, however, the developing nations are not really much better off. They note that while the prices of their commodities have perhaps quadrupled, so have those of the machinery, equipment, fertilizers and other manufactured goods they need to import. Like the rest of us, they have been affected by inflation. And most of them are living on borrowed money, the interest rates on which have risen to unprecedented levels. Several years ago the point was passed at which the annual amount of interest on loans equalled the amount given to the developed countries in aid. After that, the western nations were in the position of claiming back more than they were handing out. Like a squirrel in a cage, the developing nations had to work harder and harder to stay in the same place.

Meantime the third world's share of world trade tends to diminish steadily.

5

ACHIEVEMENTS — BUT WHAT NEXT?

Room for Encouragement

We must seek encouragement from what has been already achieved, or we would never have the heart to continue.

In the great bay of Haiti, seventy miles out from Port-au-Prince, lies the rocky island of La Gonave. Around 1964 Christians on the mainland became disturbed by the number of people who were coming over from the island and selling their children because they could not afford to keep them. You could buy a little boy for a bag of meal or a little girl for a dollar. Ostensibly the children were taken into service, but who knows?

A church minister went over to La Gonave and found the island harassed by drought, its people starving. Indeed, when four or five years later I visited the island and was asked what recommendations I would make about it, I felt inclined to answer that the only feasible solution was to abandon it. But there was nowhere on the overcrowded mainland for the people to go.

After the preliminary investigation in 1964 the church took a hand on La Gonave. A dedicated layman, Gabriel Nicholas, who was in the government agricultural service, requested that the island be put into his territory. Some of his colleagues thought he was mad to land himself with such a thankless task when he could have had a much easier life almost anywhere else.

In the years between 1964 and 1968 much was achieved. A school-cum-church was built. Concrete stores for seeds and for clinical supplies were erected. There was a house for a teacher, and little guest-room for

12. A primitive water-hole on the barren island of
La Gonave, Haiti.

visiting doctors, nurses and agriculturists. A wharf was constructed, and a
co-operative farming venture organized. Above all, a reservoir with a
capacity of 140,000 gallons was installed. Before the provision of this
water supply many villagers had to undertake a journey of two hours each
way to fetch a pitcher of water. When they arrived at the source, it was a
deep fissure in the hot rock, into which they had to descend for about thirty
feet to dip their vessels into the murky pool at the bottom. To be able to
turn a tap and see the clear water pouring out was to those villagers of La
Gonave a miracle.

Yet there were also setbacks. One is worth mentioning because it shows
how developments in the modern world can impinge on such a remote and
primitive community. Much of La Gonave is covered with a shield of lime-
stone rock, in which soil occurs in pockets. In such conditions the use of
modern machinery and modern methods of cultivation is difficult. A suit-

13. A sisal crop on La Gonave, Haiti.

able crop for the peasants of the island seemed to be sisal, the plants of which could be inserted individually in the soil pockets. So in the early years of development much sisal was planted.

The venture at first proved successful, and one or two good harvests were taken. Then man-made fibres were developed in the western world. Sisal was no longer wanted in such quantities as before. The bottom dropped out of the market. The peasants of La Gonave were left, after all their labour, with an unsaleable crop.

What in fact they did was to develop a weaving industry, making in particular table mats for export. That used up some, though not all of the surplus. But the experience was a disillusioning one.

Events in the neighbourhood of Chamrajnagar, in Mysore State, southern India, offer an encouraging illustration of what can be achieved through co-operation by a number of agencies.

In the mid-1960s the district was badly affected by drought. Among the worst sufferers were the silk farmers. Now it might be thought that farmers engaged in producing such a luxury product as silk, and for export at that, would be in an enviable position, but not a bit of it. Among Indian peasants they are the poorest of the poor. Not only are they at the mercy of middle-men who pay them as little as possible for their silk but also, in an emergency, unlike food producers they cannot eat their products. So over

14. A tray of silk-worms in southern India.

an area of many square miles an entire population had to rely on relief. Shiploads of food came into the distant ports, were transported up-country and were distributed in daily doles from relief centres.

It was, of course, appreciated that it was not compatible with human dignity, nor with official opinion of the rightness of things, for people to receive food without doing anything for it. So all the able-bodied peasants were set to tasks such as road-mending and bridge-building. It then occurred to someone that if the peasants were digging wells instead of repairing roads the danger of famine next time a drought threatened might be averted. So, early in 1968, a well-digging scheme was organized.

A well in India has a much greater diameter than the deep, narrow holes that serve as wells in Britain. A typical one I measured in the Chamrajnagar district was 30 feet across and 47 feet deep. It was an open tank, with flights of steps to give access to the water in the bottom. Under a 'food for work' scheme the digging of this well provided work for 20 or 30 men and women for about six months.

The well-digging programme was church-initiated, for the reason that church workers (mostly Indian deaconesses) were already on the spot, administering the distribution of relief supplies. They let it be known that any peasant who wanted a well on his land had only to apply. When I visited the district in 1969, 600 wells were completed or under construction, and there were many more in neighbouring districts.

The wells having been dug, a need for pumps so that the water could be used for irrigation became evident. The state government, impressed by what was going on, agreed to lend 75% of the price of a pump to any well-owner who wanted one. But that left 25%, which was approximately £25, still to be found by the peasant who in most instances had no capital at all. So again the church took the initiative and arranged for a bank to advance the money to any approved well-owner, against church securities deposited with the bank. So many peasants took advantage of the offer that the pump manufacturers offered the church a substantial commission on all orders that came in. What started as a purely philanthropic gesture therefore turned into a quite profitable investment, enabling the church to extend its agricultural activities still further.

Here we have an interesting example of many agencies in co-operation. Food came from America; the Indian government transported it by rail to the nearest convenient station; the state government hauled it from the station to the distribution centres, and also in due course made loans for the pumps; the banks played their part in providing the loans; the pump manufacturers co-operated in developing a new and promising market; and

15. An irrigation well in Mysore, southern India.

the church, in the middle of operations, supervised the whole project and gave it a sound basis.

It shows what can be done, but another promising scheme in one of the smaller west African countries did not work out so well.

At the request of a group of villages in an inland region a Dutch agriculturist started a scheme to cater for boys who stayed at home on the farms and so received no education. In order to give the project the best chance of success, away from interference by elders with traditional inhibitions, he persuaded the villagers to allow the boys to come away from their fathers' farms and to form a new settlement in the bush a mile or so away. The villagers co-operated admirably, helping the boys (aged from about nine to sixteen) to build houses and farm buildings and to dig wells.

The boys' farm was established as a kind of co-operative. Each boy had a small plot of land for growing his own food in the traditional manner. A much larger area was devoted to growing crops for sale, on a communal basis. A record was kept of the hours put in by each boy on the communal farm, so that any shirkers could be penalized. Most of the boys stuck to their tasks loyally, the bigger ones helping the smaller ones on their individual plots. Proceeds were shared out after harvest.

At first the project worked well. Representatives of sundry voluntary agencies working in west Africa visited it and pronounced it one of the most promising they had met. Within a few years three more similar projects were started within a radius of twenty miles or so.

After a time, the Dutch agriculturist moved on, leaving the boys' farms for a while under the control of a relatively inexperienced young colleague. Before he departed he arranged to give the head boy at the chief farm, on whom much responsibility rested, a small salary. It was a fatal decision.

As soon as he was out of the way, the other boys all went to his successor and demanded that they too should be paid a salary. As he naturally had no power or funds to give them money, even if he had wanted to, he refused. Whereupon they went on strike. They threw down their tools, went home and never returned. Many apparently left their villages and drifted down to the towns.

At my last visit, the land was being cultivated by a few mature farmers who had moved in and were being helped by the European team who had inherited the project. Two of the satellite schemes were still in existence but operating under difficulties. Strikes, cajolery, blackmail and black magic had all been tried to part the white men from the money which they obviously had. No doubt a mistake had been made at the beginning by giving too much. Materials, kerosene, salt, equipment, palm oil, bullocks —

all had been provided by project funds. Even broken utensils had been replaced free of charge. The farmers themselves had not invested anything except their labour in the farms; therefore when they packed up and left they lost nothing.

Yet, in spite of every discouragement, there were sufficient positive results for the project to be continued, learning from past errors.

That is the inevitable conclusion one arrives at in considering almost every scheme for rural development in the third world. In spite of frequent disappointments, there is a sufficient leavening of successes to sustain hope.

But there remains one further dilemma which becomes evident when we look at those very successes. In Kenya an enterprising young farmer who started by borrowing money to buy one cow had, when last I visited his district, acquired eleven milking cows, several followers, a flock of sheep and about 46 acres of land, on which he was practising such modern methods as the zero-grazing of lucerne, i.e. cutting the plants and carting them to the livestock rather than the more wasteful system of free grazing. In southern India a farmer who had been a coolie had acquired about 5 acres of land, 2 of which were devoted to mulberry bushes for feeding silk-worms. A well had been sunk on his land, allowing him to employ irrigation, and he was doing very well.

Near Hyderabad an Indian farmer with capital, a good education and a training in dairying in Denmark has a farm of over 50 acres on which he keeps 30 or more milking cows, mostly of European types, which yield about 600 gallons of milk per lactation — rather low by western standards but immeasurably better than most Indian cows achieve. He irrigates his land and grows immense crops of maize to feed his cattle.

Large-scale Farming

On page 55 we noted the experimental scheme at Lanet, in Kenya, where it has been established that, given a suitable diet, the lean cattle that wander down with the nomadic tribes from the Ethiopian frontier can put on flesh more quickly and more economically than can cattle of European types. It is only a matter of time before beef feedlots on the American style are established over much of tropical Africa.

We noted too that between the demonstration and experimental farms established in so many of the developing countries and the tiny peasant farms that exist all around them there seems to be an almost insuperable rampart. What goes on in the well-equipped and efficient modern farm apparently makes no impact on the peasant.

It is therefore a temptation to dismiss the government farm as an ir-relevant showpiece; but what if reality is the other way round? What if the future lies with the sophisticated modern unit? What if it is the peasant who is irrelevant?

Once we begin to think along these lines we soon see that the idea is logical. In every western country during the present century the *number* of farms and farmers has declined while the farms have grown progressively larger and more productive. In England, the peasant farmer is a figure of the past. Agriculture is now largely in the hands of farming companies often engaged in the mass production of some speciality. Farmers and farm work-ers comprise only a tiny proportion of the country's labour force.

Such big units have several advantages. They can provide ample capital for employing the most up-to-date methods and purchasing the most modern equipment, much of which is now exceedingly expensive. And they have the advantage of every mass-producing industry, namely that by producing an enormous number of units they can accept a smaller profit per unit. Table poultry units, for instance, operate on profit margins of only a few pence per bird. This is feasible for a farmer producing 100,000 table poultry in a single batch but not for one with only 40. In the 1960s profit margins on growing grain in Canada were so small that out on the prairies, far from markets, a farm of 1,000 acres was too small to provide a family with a good living. In California I have seen farms so large that fixed-winged planes have been sowing rice in the flooded fields. Yet on these units production was so economic that California could export rice to drought-stricken regions of the east — the traditional lands of paddy fields.

The Masai of east Africa are recognizing the attractions of large-scale cattle rearing. In India much black-market and other money is now being invested in farms. An Indian farm of 100 acres can provide a good standard of living for its owner, produce much food at a profit, and it offers the advantage that farmers pay no income tax!

Larger units operating by modern methods therefore have the edge over small peasant farms. They can produce more food at more competitive prices. If we take one block of 100 acres of Indian land and give it to an efficient farmer using modern methods; and if we take another block of 100 acres and leave it in the hands of its present occupiers, probably 40 or 50 of them; which will be the better, solely from the point of view of food production? Almost certainly the block under one ownership. Logically, then, if we wish to solve the world's food problem, we should take the other 100 acres from the 40 or 50 families now in occupation and give them to the first man.

The question then arises, what will the dispossessed peasants do?

It is with this dilemma that the developing nations are grappling. When I was last in west Africa the parliament of one small nation was debating a proposed law that would have made the introduction of any more labour-saving machinery a penal offence! 'Why should we want to save labour?' argued some of the delegates. 'It is the one commodity of which we have a surplus.'

The law was not passed, and most countries are trying instead to copy the example of the west. England moved away from a peasant economy through the throes of the Industrial Revolution, in the course of which factories offered alternative employment to work on the land. Many nations are now doing the same. Examples are Japan, Taiwan and South Korea. But many others have little hope of solving their problems in that way during the present generation. And even the developed countries are now plagued with doubts. Automation has progressed so far that modern factories can be run with the services of a handful of men. There may never again be enough work available to provide full employment for everyone.

So the developing world is faced with the quandary that if it sets out to solve its food production problems by stimulating efficient farming it will almost inevitably have on its hands still more millions of dispossessed and unemployed peasants. These are the people who will need the food, and they will have no money to buy it.

The Population Problem

If drastic steps such as these were to be taken, could the world be fed?

It is in fact technically possible to provide adequate food for the 4,000 million or so people in the world at present. It would also be possible to feed, though doubtless with greater difficulty, the 7,000 million inhabitants which the world is expected to have to support by the year AD 2000.

But beyond that all is darkness. Such a population at the end of the century will demonstrate that the world population has taken only thirty years to double itself. The time required for it to double itself again will be less, as simple arithmetic will show. Can the world food supply be doubled at an equivalent rate? Or can the brake be applied adequately to the birth-rate?

Clearly absolute priority ought now to be given to the problems raised in this book. The necessary increases in food supplies demand fairer systems of trade and aid, the development of appropriate technologies for rural agriculture, and the general improvement of rural areas. But will even that be enough? Somewhere there has to be a point where maximum production will be reached. How can we ensure that at that point the population will stop increasing?